Eliete Pereira Viturino
Ana Lucia Mª.da S.Gomes

Evaluation of students' knowledge of amphibians and reptiles

AF154713

Eliete Pereira Viturino
Ana Lucia Mª.da S.Gomes

Evaluation of students' knowledge of amphibians and reptiles

A review

ScienciaScripts

This book is a translation from the original published under ISBN 978-613-9-60170-7.

Publisher:
Sciencia Scripts
is a trademark of
Dodo Books Indian Ocean Ltd. and OmniScriptum S.R.L publishing group

120 High Road, East Finchley, London, N2 9ED, United Kingdom
Str. Armeneasca 28/1, office 1, Chisinau MD-2012, Republic of Moldova, Europe
Printed at: see last page
ISBN: 978-620-7-27041-5

ACKNOWLEDGEMENTS

To my parents, Maria Filomena Gomes and Adauto José da Silva, for their encouragement, love and understanding.

To my siblings, Andréia Maria da Silva Gomes, Ana Regina Gomes, Marta Rita Gomes, Adriana Gomes da Silva, Murilo Alex Gomes da Silva...

To all the teachers who were present during my academic career, especially my supervisor Eliete Pereira Viturino and co-supervisor Ana Paula Gomes, for their patience and dedication, which were essential to the completion of this work.

To the professors who are no longer part of the FAOPST faculty for sharing their knowledge with us.

To AESET/FAFOPST for the availability of professionals and the service provided.

To the University for All Programme in Pernambuco (PROUPE) for the scholarship, which enabled me to complete the course.

"There is no such thing as knowing more or knowing less: there is different knowledge."

PAULO FREIRE

SUMMARY

Herpetology is the science dedicated to the study of amphibians and reptiles. Individuals belonging to this group are popularly known as cold-blooded animals, i.e. ectotherms. Amphibians are animals that have different life stages, one aquatic and the other terrestrial, restricting themselves to humid environments to ensure their survival. They are carnivorous animals, feeding on insects and other small arthropods. They play an important biological role in nature as pest controllers and nutrient dispersers in aquatic environments. Unlike amphibians, reptiles can colonise different environments, including aquatic ones, and their dry skin covered in scales guarantees a wider range of habitats. Most of these individuals are top predators. In addition to their carnivorous habits, they also have herbivorous individuals such as iguanas. For humans, reptiles also have a socio-economic character, as they serve as food and a source of research in the pharmaceutical industry, such as snake venom for the production of medicines. Despite the current times, many legends circulate in the human imagination, especially about snakes. This situation ends up leading to the extermination of these animals, causing a certain environmental and even public health imbalance. The aim of this research was to analyse the knowledge that public school students in Serra Talhada have about amphibians and reptiles, especially with regard to their classification, biology and ecological importance. A semi-structured questionnaire was used to carry out the research, and the data obtained was compiled in Excel spreadsheets which served as a tool for producing tables and graphs. According to the results obtained, it can be seen that the participants in the research have considerable knowledge about amphibians and reptiles, however, there is still the influence of certain legends that make up this learning, and it is necessary to elucidate these themes within the science disciplines, especially in the early grades, as well as bringing students closer to the reality that surrounds them, through changes in the profile of science classes, confronting scientific and traditional knowledge.

Keywords: Herpetology. Ethnozoology. Ethnoherpetology.

SUMMARY

CHAPTER 1

INTRODUCTION

Herpetology is one of the branches of zoology dedicated to understanding and classifying amphibians and reptiles biologically. Individuals belonging to this group are popularly known as cold-blooded animals, i.e. ectotherms (BERNARDE, 2012; LUCHESE, 2013).

Associated with herpetology, ethnoherpetology is restricted to researching the interaction between human beings and the aforementioned group, mainly with regard to traditional knowledge (BARBOSA et al., 2007).

Amphibians are animals that have different life stages, one aquatic and the other terrestrial, restricting themselves to humid environments to ensure their survival. The origin of amphibians dates back to the Devonian period, around 350 million years ago. They are carnivorous animals, feeding on insects and other small arthropods (DUELLMAN and TRUEB, 1994; SANTOS et al., 2013). They play an important biological role in nature as pest controllers and nutrient dispersers in aquatic environments. Unlike amphibians, reptiles can colonise different environments, including aquatic ones, and their dry skin covered in scales ensures a wider range of habitat expansion. Most of these individuals are top-of-the-chain animals, i.e. predators (HICKMAN et al., 2004; STORER et al., 2010; SANTOS et al., 2013).

In addition to their carnivorous habits, they also have herbivorous individuals such as iguanas. For humans, reptiles also have a socio-economic character, as they serve as food and a source of research in the pharmaceutical industry, such as snake venom for the production of medicines (MARTINS et al., 2003; BERNARDE, 2012).

Brazil has a great herpetological diversity with 732 species of reptiles and 946 species of amphibians. In the northeast, especially in the caatinga, there is also considerable biodiversity for the group in question, with greater relevance for reptiles with 152 catalogued species (RODRIGUES, 2003; BERNARDE, 2012; SANTOS et al., 2013).

Despite the current times, many legends circulate in the human imagination, especially about snakes. This situation ends up leading to the extermination of these animals, causing a certain environmental and even public health imbalance, and these problems could be solved with more effective environmental preservation measures (BARBOSA et al., 2010). Bearing in mind that herpetology is a little-studied term, the aim of this research was to analyse the knowledge that public school students in Serra Talhada have about amphibians

4

and reptiles, especially with regard to classification and biology, ecological importance, as well as attitudes towards mistreatment.

CHAPTER 2

THEORETICAL FRAMEWORK

2.1 HERPETOLOGY

Zoology is the science dedicated to the study of animal life, which requires years of research and investigation by man into its biology, genetics, physiology, anatomy, ecology and evolution (HICKMAN et al., 2004).

Herpetology is the branch of zoology dedicated to the study of amphibians and reptiles, from classification to evolution (BERNARDE, 2012;LUCHESE, 2013). Amphibians and reptiles are tetrapod vertebrates, animals characterised by the presence of four legs, which also include birds and mammals. These animals do not produce their own heat and are popularly called cold-blooded animals (ectotherms) and although they are not evolutionarily close to each other, they are grouped together due to the similarity of their study techniques (HICKMAN et al., 2004).

This field has recently gained strength in Brazil and, since 2004, herpetologists from all over Brazil have met at the Brazilian Congress of Herpetology every two years. "Herpetology has grown a lot in recent years, but a lot still needs to be done, as there are several areas that are under-sampled or where practically no surveys have been carried out," says Bernarde (2012, p.14).

In contrast, ethnobiology is the science that studies the interactions between humans and other living beings. Among the branches of this science are ethnozoology and ethnoherpetology, both of which cover specific subjects. The former studies man's traditional knowledge of animals, focusing on the interaction processes between each society and its local fauna (MOURA et al., 2010), while the latter studies man's traditional knowledge of amphibians and reptiles, as well as the relationship between them (BARBOSA et al., 2007).

In this context, ethnozoology is the multidisciplinary study of the relationships between human cultures and animals (COSTA-NETO, 2000). It is therefore the transdisciplinary study of thoughts and perceptions (knowledge and beliefs), feelings and behaviours that mediate relations between human populations (SANTOS-FITA et al., 2007).

2.1.1 The Herpetofauna of the Caatinga

The caatinga is the only biome restricted to Brazilian territory, basically occupying the Northeast Region, with some areas in the state of Minas Gerais (LEAL et al., 2003). It is

6

known as a semi-arid savannah, with higher and more accentuated temperatures and potential evapotranspiration, which further aggravates the effects of low and irregular rainfall. It resembles the Cerrado savannah biome and is also formed by a complex of physiognomic forms distributed in a mosaic, such as arboreal caatinga, shrubby caatinga, thorny caatinga, etc. (ANDRADE-LIMA, 1966; 1981). The herpetofauna of the northeastern semi-arid region is still a recent field of study, initially consisting of rather diffuse information for particular regions, corresponding to species lists and records of sparse collections in space and time (BORGES-NORJOSA &SANTOS, 2005).

Brazil ranks second in the world for reptile diversity, with around 732 species, second only to Australia (BERNARDE, 2012; SANTOS et al., 2013). Of these, 152 are found in the Caatinga Biome, distributed among 44 species of lizards, nine of amphibenids, 47 of snakes, four of chelonians and three of crocodilians (SANTOS et al., 2013; RODRIGUES, 2003).There are currently around 6,240 amphibian species catalogued in the tropics and temperate regions. In Brazil, there are approximately 946 species of amphibians, distributed in 1 caudata, 27 Gymnophiona and 918 Anuros. Of this total, 52 amphibian species are found in the caatinga biome, where they have a high degree of endemism. In Pernambuco, around 20 species have been described and among the most studied areas are the municipalities of Serra Talhada, Buíque and Ouricuri (SANTOS et al., 2013).

2.2 EVOLUTION AND GENERAL CHARACTERISTICS OF THE AMPHIBIA GROUP

Amphibians colonised the terrestrial environment in the Devonian period around 350 million years ago and have intermediate characteristics between fish and terrestrial amniotes, with significant morphological and ecological evolution. They have the greatest diversity of ways of life of any other group of vertebrates (DUELLMAN &TRUEB,1994).

Amphibians, as their name suggests (amphi = two; bio = life) are animals that have a transition from water to land, in other words, they have two phases in their life cycle, one aquatic and one terrestrial and, thanks to these characteristics, they are considered to be the first animals to inhabit the terrestrial environment (HICKMAN et al., 2004).Without a shadow of a doubt, these animals derive from a fish-like ancestor that lived in the Devonian period. However, this transition involved physiological and physical changes, such as the replacement of fins with legs, changes to the skin to facilitate breathing and the replacement of gills with lungs in adults. There were also changes in metabolism and excretion, where they began to produce fewer toxic excreta and obtained sense organs that function both in water and on land (STORER et al., 2010). This transition was therefore a landmark event in animal evolution, and is the main point that links amphibians to other vertebrate groups

7

(HICKMAN et al., 2004).

They live partly in fresh water or in humid places and can be found in temperate and humid regions, but most are tropical (STORER et al., 2010). They are carnivorous animals and feed on a vast diversity of insects and small arthropods, which is why it is worth emphasising the importance of these animals for the environment. They act as pest controllers and indicators of environmental quality (SANTOS et al., 2013), since they have extremely sensitive skin, which also makes them vulnerable to climatic and environmental changes, such as alterations to the rainfall cycle and pollution (LUCHESE, 2013). They act as dispersers in the nutrient cycle in freshwater lakes, as their larvae transport these nutrients to the land once they have metamorphosed. They serve as food for various animals, including humans, and many species are used in biology teaching and research (STORER et al., 2010).

The class is represented by three orders: Anura, Caudata and Gymnophiona (SANTOS et al., 2013). The Anura order is represented by frogs and toads, which have elongated hind legs and an inflexible body that doesn't bend when they walk; the Caudata order is represented by salamanders, which have front and hind legs of equal size and move by lateral undulations; the Gymnophiona order is represented by cecilians, which have no legs and move similarly to snakes (MAFFEI, 2010).

2.3 EVOLUTION AND CHARACTERISTICS OF THE REPTILIA GROUP

The first group of vertebrates to inhabit the terrestrial environment were the reptiles, effectively adapted to life in dry places, although some representatives of this group are aquatic. They are more advanced than the amphibians, having dry, impermeable skin covered by epidermal scales (in snakes and lizards), horny plates (in crocodilians) and also bony plates (turtles). They have an ossified skeleton, internal fertilisation and eggs with shells, adapted for development in a dry environment. They are ectothermic, i.e. they are unable to produce their own heat and depend on external sources for warmth (STORER et al., 2010).Reptiles inhabit different types of environments, including aquatic ones. The earth already harboured giant reptile forms around 165 million years ago during the period known as the Age of Reptiles, which witnessed an incredible variety of aquatic and terrestrial forms, including the giant herbivorous and carnivorous dinosaurs (HICKMAN et al., 2004).

The characteristic scales of reptiles are basically made up of keratin and are derived from the epidermis, making them homologous to those of fish, i.e. they have the same structure but different functions. In some reptiles, such as alligators, the scales remain for life, growing continuously as they wear down, while in snakes and lizards, new scales grow

8

under the old ones, which are replaced periodically. In snakes, the older skin (epidermis and scales) is turned inside out when it is discarded, while lizards release the old skin intact and with the outside facing out, and it can sometimes be left in pieces. Turtles have flattened shields that are modified scales, which add new layers of keratin beneath the older layers of their shield as they grow (HICKMAN et al., 2004).

The evolutionary separation between amphibians and reptiles basically came about with the appearance of the shelled egg, and this adaptation contributed to the evolutionary establishment of reptiles. Internal fertilisation was essential for the appearance of a shelled egg, as the sperm must reach the egg before it is enveloped by the shell (HICKMAN et al., 2004).

The lungs of reptiles are more developed than those of amphibians, which depend almost exclusively on their lungs for gas exchange. In some aquatic turtles, breathing is supplemented by pharyngeal mucous membranes and, unlike amphibians, which force air into their lungs with the help of their mouth muscles, reptiles suck air into their lungs by expanding their ribcage (snakes and lizards) or by moving their internal organs (turtles and crocodilians). Reptiles do not have a muscular diaphragm, a structure exclusive to mammals (HICKMAN et al., 2004).

According to Martins and Molina (2003), reptiles occur in practically all Brazilian ecosystems and, because they are ectothermic, they are especially diverse and abundant in the warmer regions of the country. Thus, our greatest diversity of reptiles is found in the Amazon, the Atlantic Rainforest, the Cerrado and the Caatinga.

A large proportion of these animals are predators, often at the top of the food chain. Alligators and many snakes are good examples. Other reptiles such as amphisbaenians, most lizards, some snakes and some turtles are secondary consumers, feeding mainly on insects. There are also some lizards and turtles that are herbivores, acting as primary consumers in trophic chains. In addition to folivorous species such as iguanas, several other lizards consume fruit and can act as dispersers for various plant species. Because they often occur in relatively high densities, these animals play a very important role in the functioning of Brazilian ecosystems.

In addition to their ecological importance, several reptile species also have socio-economic importance, especially some chelonians, which serve as food for human populations, and venomous snakes, whose venoms give rise to medicines that are widely used in Brazil and around the world (MARTINS et al., 2003; BERNARDEZ, 2012), The venom of the common jararaca, *Bothrops jararaca, has given rise to* medicines such as the antihypertensive Captopril (MARTINS et al., 2003; BERNARDE, 2012), and EVAS IN, which was recently patented by researchers at the Butantan Institute in São Paulo. Another new product is ENPAK, a protein with analgesic power, obtained from the venom of the rattlesnake, *Crotalusterrificus,* whose effect may be 600 times more powerful than that of Morphine (BÉRNILSet al., 2004).

Therefore, the conservation of Brazilian venomous snakes will also preserve the pharmaceutical and socio-economic potential of their venoms.

2.4 TRADITIONAL KNOWLEDGE ABOUT AMPHIBIANS AND REPTILES

Among the approaches that have contributed most to empirical study are ethnosciences, such as ethnobiology, which is the scientific study of the dynamics of the relationship between people and their cultural groups and the environment, from the distant past to the immediate present (ROCHA-COELHO, 2009). Ethnobiology essentially consists of the study of knowledge and conceptualisations developed by man about biology, i.e. the study of the role of nature in man's system of beliefs and adaptations to certain environments (POSEY, 1987).

According to Adams (2000, p.119), this science: "values the knowledge accumulated by traditional populations, provides important arguments for the preservation of these peoples and their habitats, as well as for the creation of socially and ecologically fairer policies".

Some authors show the importance of studying traditional knowledge, such as:

According to Martins Neto (2011), the ethnoherpetological knowledge of the inhabitants of the city of Patos, in the hinterland mesoregion of the state of Paraíba, promoted a survey of popular knowledge in relation to the stories widely disseminated in this environment. This work showed that popular knowledge is vast and that this knowledge is often made up of information that does not tally with the published literature on these animals. It was also observed that this knowledge is mostly passed down among family members.

In his book, Amphibians and reptiles: an introduction to the study of Brazilian herpetofauna, Bernarde (2012, p. 205), dedicates a chapter exclusively to legends and beliefs about snakes in various regions of Brazil, stating that "it is important for herpetologists to know a little about this subject", the author also argues that the way people see these animals is related to their conservation, since they live together with amphibians and reptiles. In addition, he emphasises that "in order to want to preserve them, you have to have a certain sympathy or even a liking for these animals; demystifying beliefs that worsen the image of amphibians and reptiles and highlighting the importance of these animals

(BERNARDE, 2012.p. 205).

Fernandes-Ferreira and colleagues (2011) carried out an ethnographic survey of beliefs and their respective scientific inferences involving ophidians in the state of Ceará, in north-eastern Brazil. The research was carried out between 2008 and 2010. In this study, the researchers stated that in the areas they visited there is a differentiation between snakes with and without venom, and that most of the snakes considered venomous by the interviewees do not have lethal venomous potential for human beings.

Barbosa and colleagues (2010) sought to assess the ethnoherpetological knowledge of the community of Serra de Joaquim Vieira, located in São José da Mata (a district of Campina Grande - Paraíba) and to analyse the relationship between humans *and* reptiles. In this work, the authors found a close human/reptile relationship in the community as well as the use of these animals as a source of food and zootherapies.

For certain species of snakes, beliefs were raised consisting of assimilations of morphological, physiological and ecological characters, most of which do not corroborate zoological literature. It was realised that this is probably because the feeling of fear prevents an approach that could promote popular knowledge that more consistently corroborates scientific knowledge.

The conflicting relationship between humans and snakes leads to a layman's justification for the indiscriminate slaughter of these animals, causing serious environmental and public health problems, which must be solved mainly through public policies for environmental education, prevention and treatment of snakebite accidents.

In association, the conservation of herpetofauna and ethnozoological studies can help to assess whether the populations of some species are being overexploited, which can cause their decline or even extinction in certain places.

2.505 KNOWLEDGE ACQUIRED IN BASIC EDUCATION

Basic education in Brazil has become quite complex in the years since the 1988 Federal Constitution, and the factors that determine it have been the subject of national laws, policies and programmes, some of which are in agreement with international bodies (KURY, 2002).

According to Law No. 9.394 of 20 December 1996, Art. 1

> Education encompasses the formative processes that take place in family life, in human coexistence, at work, in educational and research institutions, in social movements and civil society organisations, and in cultural manifestations.

11

According to Law 9.394, basic education is made up of early childhood education, primary education and secondary education. It is the only compulsory stage of education and constitutes the basis of academic training in our country. Its basic aims are to develop the student, ensure that he or she has the common and indispensable training to exercise citizenship, and provide him or her with the means to progress in work and further studies.

According to Rosa (2009), the knowledge learnt in primary school is the only learning about the biological sciences that students acquire, and it plays an essential role in raising awareness and building values for life.

Secondary education is the final stage of basic education, lasting at least three years, and one of its aims is to deepen the knowledge acquired in the previous grades, as well as to prepare students for work and citizenship (LDB, 2004).

Article 208(I) of the 1988 constitution guarantees access to free primary education, including for those who did not have access to it at the right age. This constitutional provision therefore determines the state's duty to promote youth and adult education.

Youth and Adult Education is a type of primary and secondary education, giving young people and adults the opportunity to start and/or continue their studies. In 1996, the Law of Guidelines and Bases defined that youth and adult education should meet the interests and needs of individuals who already had a certain life experience, participate in the world of work and therefore have a very different education from the children and adolescents for whom regular education is intended. This is why Youth and Adult Education is also understood as continuous and permanent education.

In this way, the national curriculum parameters - PCNs - were drawn up with the aim of adding the regional, cultural and political diversities of Brazilian students to the need to build common national references for the teaching of the various subjects and areas of knowledge in basic schools (BRASIL, 1997).

The national curriculum parameters for secondary education are divided into: Languages, Codes and their Technologies; Natural Sciences, Mathematics and their Technologies; Human Sciences and their Technologies. The area of Natural Sciences is divided into four thematic axes: 1) Life and the Environment; 2) Human Beings and Health; 3) Technology and Society; 4) Earth and the Universe (BRASIL, 1997, 2000).

They can also act as a catalyst for action to improve the quality of Brazilian education, but in no way are they intended to solve all the problems that affect the quality of teaching and learning in the country, which imposes the need for investment on different fronts, such as initial and continuing teacher training, a decent salary policy, a career plan, the quality of textbooks, television and multimedia resources, and the availability of teaching materials.

But this desired qualification also implies placing school teaching and learning activities at the centre of the debate, as well as the issue of curriculum, as being of undeniable importance to the educational policy of the Brazilian nation (BRASIL, 1997).

The school is a privileged space for establishing connections and information, as one of the possibilities for creating conditions and alternatives that encourage students to have citizen conceptions and attitudes, aware of their responsibilities and, above all, to perceive themselves as members of the environment. Formal education remains an important space for developing values and attitudes committed to ecological and social sustainability (LIMA, 2004).

According to Chalita (2002), education is the most powerful of all the tools for intervening in the world to build new concepts and consequently change habits. It is also the instrument for building knowledge and the way in which all the intellectual development achieved is passed on from one generation to the next, thus enabling the proven maxim of each generation moving one step ahead of the previous one in the field of scientific and general knowledge.

In the view of Dias (2004), environmental education at school should not be conservationist, i.e. one whose teachings lead to the rational use of natural resources and the maintenance of an optimum level of productivity of natural ecosystems or those managed by man, but one that focuses on the environment and implies a profound change in values, a new world view, which goes far beyond the conservationist state.

Biodiversity conservation is one of the essential components for sustainability in its ecological, economic and socio-cultural dimensions (OLIVEIRA, 2004; RODRIGUES, 2001). In this context, it can be said that Environmental Education is a strategy used in biodiversity conservation actions (RODRIGUES, 2007).

CHAPTER 3

METHODOLOGY

3.1 CHARACTERISATION OF THE RESEARCH

This research is an investigation into the knowledge of amphibians and reptiles acquired during the final stages of Youth and Adult Education and is based on a qualitative and quantitative approach (LAKATOS, 2003; GIL, 2006) in which the focus is on the meanings, thoughts and ideas that the participants attribute to the subject (MINAYO, 2012).

This research can be classified as field and bibliographical research, which according to Gil (2008, p.50) "is based on material that has already been prepared, consisting mainly of books and scientific articles". Field research, according to Prestes (2008, p. 27), "is research in which the researcher, using a questionnaire [...] collects data, investigating those being researched in their environment". It is also descriptive and exploratory. Regarding this classification, Gil (2008, p. 27) reveals: its main purpose is to develop, clarify and modify concepts and ideas, with a view to formulating more precise problems or researchable hypotheses for subsequent studies [...] It usually involves a bibliographical and documentary survey, non-standardised interviews and case studies.

As for descriptive research, Gil (2008, p.28) explains: "The primary objective of descriptive research is to describe the characteristics of a given population or phenomenon or to establish relationships between variables."

In order to achieve the objectives proposed in this research, a qualitative approach was also used, as suggested by Bardin (1977, p. 21):

> In quantitative analysis, it is the presence or absence of a given content characteristic or set of characteristics in a given message fragment that is taken into account.

In this way, the data collected (opinions, information) was translated into numbers and is therefore considered quantifiable, making it necessary to use statistical techniques such as ratios, proportions, percentages and rates. Tables and graphs will be used to present the data. Marconi and Lakatos (2011, p.112) state that: "The data collected by the research will be presented in **raw form**, requiring the use of statistics for its arrangement, analysis and understanding".

In this context, Barros (2001, p.72) adds: "Finally, to select the measuring instrument, relate the technical instrument you know and know how to use to what you want to measure. Consider the basic principles of validity, reliability and precision".

3.2 THE AREA STUDIED

Serra Talhada is a Brazilian municipality belonging to the state of Pernambuco, located in the upper Pajeú micro-region, in the northern part of the state of Pernambuco, geographically bordered to the north by the state of Paraíba, to the south by Floresta, to the east by Calumbi, Betânia and Santa Cruz da Baixa Verde, and to the west by São José do Belmonte and Mirandiba (Figure 1). It belongs to the caatinga biome and is bathed by the Pajeú river. The city is popularly known as the Capital of Xaxado, and is approximately 415 kilometres from the capital of Pernambuco, Recife (FCCST, 2012). The city has a significant educational centre, with public schools, public schools, full-time schools and technical schools, as well as higher education institutions (BRASIL, 2008). Its land area is 2,980 km² and the population is around 79,232 (IBGE, 2010).The caatinga is the only biome restricted to Brazilian territory, basically occupying the Northeast Region, with some areas in the state of Minas Gerais (LEAL et al., 2003). It is known as a semi-arid savannah, with higher and more accentuated temperatures and potential evapotranspiration, which further aggravates the effects of low and irregular rainfall. It resembles the Cerrado savannah biome and is also formed by a complex of physiognomic forms distributed in a mosaic, such as arboreal caatinga, shrubby caatinga, thorny caatinga, etc. (ANDRADE- LIMA, 1966; 1981).

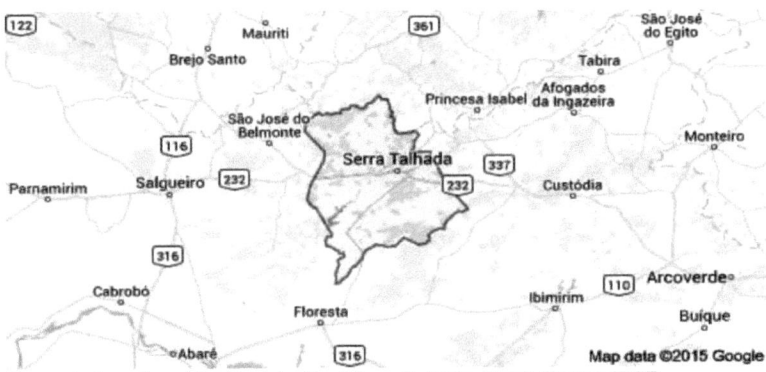

Figure 1 - Location of the Municipality of Serra Talhada, Brazil. Source: IBGE.

3.3 RESEARCH UNIVERSE AND SAMPLE

According to Lakatos and Gil (2003, p. 223), the universe or population of a research comprises "the set of animate or inanimate beings that have at least one characteristic in

15

common". Therefore, the universe of this research was made up of 18 students from the 3rd[a] phase and 23 students from the 4th[a] phase of the EJA at the CT school, 26 students from the 2nd module and 22 students from the 3rd module of the EJA at the SL school, totalling 89 students from the CT and SL schools, from the evening shift, of both genders, aged between 18 and 55.

According to Lakatos (2011, p. 112), the sample "constitutes a portion or parcel conveniently selected from the universe (population); it is a subset of the universe". According to the premise, the sample of this research in relation to the number of the universe, will be 29 students, being 6 students of the 3rd phase and 7 students of the 4th phase of the EJA of the CT school, 8 students of the 2nd module and 8 students of the 3rd module of the EJA of the SL school.

3.4 INCLUSION CRITERIA

- Students duly enrolled in schools ;
- Be male or female;
- Those who agreed to take part in the research and signed the Free and Informed Consent Form;
- Students aged 18 or over.

3.5 Exclusion criteria

- Students under the age of 18, even if they are enrolled in EJA;
- Students who refused to take part in the research and did not sign the Free and Informed Consent Form;
- Students who left the classroom at the time of the survey;
- Absent students;
- Students who refused to answer the questionnaire for any reason;

3.6 THE PARTICIPATING SCHOOLS

The schools taking part in this research are municipal and state public schools, respectively, both in the city of Serra Talhada - PE.

3.7 DATA COLLECTION AND ANALYSIS

16

The first stage of the research consisted of choosing two public schools, one state and one municipal, both belonging to the municipality of Serra Talhada. In order to achieve the objectives proposed in this research, bibliographic consultation was used, as well as the application of a questionnaire, which sought to address a little about reproduction, feeding and living habits, as well as attitudes and perceptions regarding amphibians and reptiles.

The first contact was in person, where the objectives of the research were explained to the management of both schools, and after the management agreed, we went to the classrooms to invite the students interested to take part in the research and hand them the informed consent form to sign. For ethical reasons, it was stated in the body of the form that the names of those involved, as well as the participating institutions, would be kept confidential, as shown in Annex 02. Afterwards, the structured questionnaire was administered, containing open and closed questions, according to Boni & Quaresma (2005). We chose to carry out the research with young people and adults in the final stages, as a guarantee that they had all studied living beings at some point in the previous grades, even if they came from different schools. They answered the questionnaires individually and without the help of teachers, classmates or books.

The data obtained was compiled in Excel spreadsheets, which served as a tool for producing tables and graphs. The objective questions were corrected and analysed qualitatively through comparisons between proportions. The answers to the individual questions were copied exactly as written, to avoid losing details or expressions, and then analysed in an exploratory descriptive manner according to Gil (2008).

CHAPTER 4

RESULTS AND DISCUSSION

4.1 THE STUDENTS

Of the 29 students who took part in this research, 15 were female14 and 15 were male. Of these 29, 13 were from school A and 16 from school B.

Of the 13 participants from school A, 6 are from the third stage and 7 from the fourth stage of primary EJA. Of the 16 students from school B, 8 are from the second module and 8 from the third module, which correspond to the second and third year, respectively, of secondary education.

4.1.1 The questionnaire

The questionnaire for this research, containing 10 open and closed (objective) questions, was based on bibliographical references, as well as the proposed objectives, where 2 to 3 questions were drawn up for each objective, as shown in Table 1, which sought to cover a little about diversity, biology, popular beliefs, feelings and values relating to amphibians and reptiles.

Table 1. Questionnaire applied to students in youth and adult education at theMUII and EST2 schools in the municipality of Serra Talhada, Pernambuco, in November 2015. In the first column, the list of questions asked, and in the second, the objectives to be explored. The correct answers to the objective questions are marked in bold (Adapted from: Luchese 2013).

QUESTION	OBJECTIVES

1) According to your knowledge, which of the animals listed below are amphibians?
  a) Cecilias and turtles
  b) Toads, frogs, turtles and turtles
  c) **Frogs, toads, salamanders and Cecilias**
  d) I don't know
	To assess the students' level of knowledge about the representatives of each group, especially in relation to two-headed snakes and cecilians, animals that are generally little known.

2) According to your knowledge, which of the animals listed below are reptiles?
  a) **Snakes, lizards, turtles, two-headed snakes and caimans**
  b) Cecilias and two-headed snakes
  c) Toads, frogs, turtles and turtles
  d) I don't know	

3) What role do amphibians and reptiles play in nature?
  a) **act as trophic controllers and bio-indicators**
  b) transmit diseases to humans
  c) pose a threat to human beings
	Evaluating the students' perception of ecological importance of the

18

d) I don't know	animals in focus.
4 Comment on what you feel when you see or hear about: Toad: Cobra: Turtle: Alligator:	To assess the degree of rejection for the two groups, as well as attitudes towards abuse
5) Have you ever seen someone mistreating this type of animal? What did you do? ( ) yes ( ) no	
6) Why do frogs sing when it rains? a)To mark their territory **b)To attract the attention of the female to start the reproduction process** c)To scare people d)I don't know	To assess students' knowledge of the biology (reproduction, feeding, etc.) of amphibians and reptiles.
7) Why do frogs and toads occur at night?	
8) What do amphibians and reptiles eat?	
9) Many frogs, snakes and lizards are brightly coloured, why is this? a) To ward off the predator b) To be used as pets c) To attract female attention d) I don't know	
10) According to your knowledge of amphibians and reptiles, mark the true alternatives with V and the false alternatives with F: ( ) The age of the rattlesnake can be measured by counting the rattle rings at the tip of the tail. ( ) Snakes can hear. **( ) The lizard, when it loses a piece of its tail, has the ability to make a new one grow.** ( ) Coral snake stings with its tail. ( ) Blind toad urine. ( ) The frog is the female of the toad.	Identify which myths are present in the students' daily lives and which facts they know/do not know.

4.1.2 Questions

When analysing the first two questions, there was a mistake in the classification of amphibians and reptiles. In the first question, 31.03% correctly identified all the amphibians, but 58.02% considered alternative *"B"* (frogs, toads, turtles and frogs) to be correct, which shows that the participants had never heard of Cecilia as an animal name. Of the remaining 10.95 per cent, 6.90 per cent couldn't answer and 3.45 per cent considered alternative *"A"* to be correct, as shown in graph 1.

According to your knowledge, which of the animals listed below are amphibians?

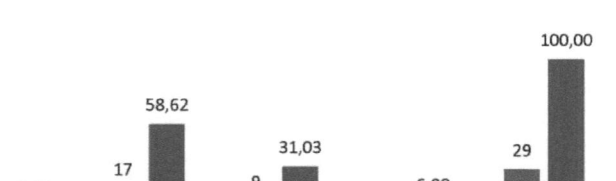

Graph 1. Knowledge of amphibians among students in Youth and Adult Education in the public school system in Serra Talhada, Pernambuco (n=29) (Question 1). Legend: A) Cecilias and turtles; B) Toads, frogs, tree frogs and turtles; C) Toads, frogs, tree frogs, salamanders and caecilians; D) I don't know.

In relation to question 2^a , 65.52% of the participants chose the correct alternative "A", snakes, **lizards, turtles, two-headed snakes and alligators,** and 17% considered the correct alternative "B" to be Cecilia and two-headed snakes. Although the majority chose the correct alternative, their knowledge of the two-headed snake as a reptile cannot be proven, as at least five participants were asked during the survey whether two-headed snakes exist, thus proving their lack of knowledge about the animal (Graph 2).

According to your knowledge, which of the animals listed below are reptiles?

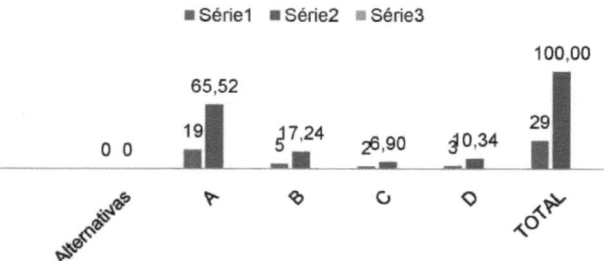

Graph 2. Knowledge of reptiles among Youth and Adult Education students from the public school system in Serra Talhada, Pernambuco (n=29) (Question 2). Legend: A) Snakes, lizards, turtles, two-headed snakes and alligators; B) Cecilias and two-headed snakes; C) Toads, frogs, turtles and turtles; D) I don't know.

Cecilias, also known as blind snakes, are amphibians belonging to the order Gymnophiona, which lack legs and move similarly to snakes (MAFFEI, 2010; BERNARDE, 2012). Cecilias have a vermiform body and a compact skull, covered in bones adapted for digging, and smooth skin with transverse grooves reminiscent of earthworms (Photo 1A). Their skin has mucous glands that discharge an irritating liquid; they also have some dermal scales implanted in the skin; a small portable tentacle between the eyes and the nostril; eyes without an eyelid, often under the skin or jawbone (Photo 1 B) (STORER et al., 2003).

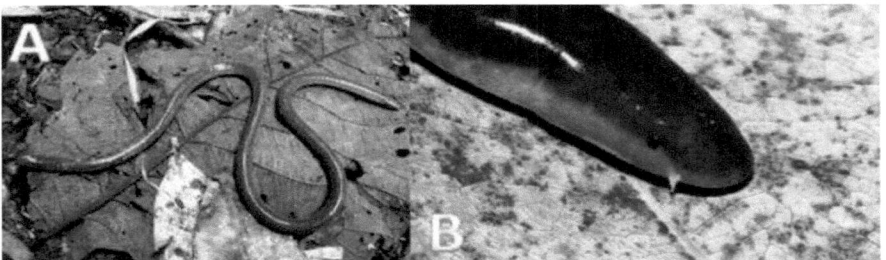

Figure 2.A. Blind snake (*Caecilia marcusi*). Photo: Paulo Sérgio Bernarde. Source: Herpetofauna.com. B. Detail of the tentacle and eyelidless eye in *Caecilia ssp.* Photo: John Measey. Source: NUROF Blog.

Amphisbaenids are Squamata (scaled) reptiles with a fossorial habit, popularly known as two-headed snakes. They are little-known animals in the urban environment, although they are present in everyday rural life. The popular name "two-headed snake" is attributed to amphisbaenids because they have a morphologically similar head and tail (Photo 2 A), corresponding to an adaptation to their burrowing habit and underground life. When it feels threatened, it puts both ends of its body in an attack position, which makes it appear to have two heads (Photo 2 B) (MATEUS et al., 2011). Mateus and his collaborators (2011) carried out an ethnobiological study in the village of Itatiaia, Minas Gerais, with the aim of recording popular knowledge and beliefs about these animals, where 48 residents of the village were interviewed. According to the number of residents who were interviewed, it can be said that the population classifies amphisbaenids as snakes, considering them to be dangerous animals and favouring their death whenever they are found.

Figure 3. A) Two-headed snake (*Amphisbaena alba*). Photo: Cristiano Nogueira. Source: Diário de Biologia; B) *A. alba* with both ends of its body raised in an attack/defence position. Photo: Raul Rodrigues. Source: Abelhas Potiguares blog

In the third question, the majority of participants (65.52%) correctly indicated that **amphibians and reptiles act as trophic controllers and bio-indicators**, alternative "A",

21

6.90% ticked alternative "B", 13.79% considered alternative "C" and a further 13.79% were unable to answer (graph 3).

What role do amphibians and reptiles play in nature?

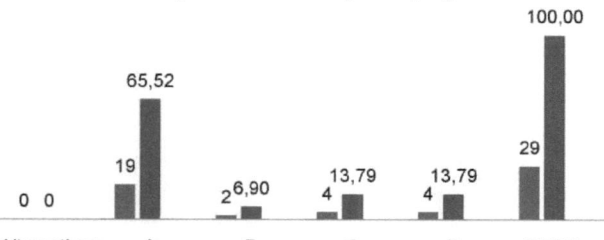

Alternativas   A   B   C   D   TOTAL

Graph 3. Recognition of the role of amphibians and reptiles in nature by students of Youth and Adult Education in the public school system of Serra Talhada, Pernambuco (n=29), (Question 3). Legend: A) Act as trophic controllers and bio-indicators; B) Transmit diseases to humans; C) Present a threat to humans; D) Don't know.

As we discussed earlier, both amphibians and reptiles act as pest controllers. Because they feed on a wide variety of insects and small arthropods, amphibians are extremely important for the balance of the food chain, because if there were no predators for certain animals, especially insects, they would become real pests, as they reproduce very quickly. Amphibians also act as indicators of environmental quality, since they have very sensitive skin, which also makes them vulnerable to climate and environmental changes (SANTOS et al., 2013).

In addition to acting as controllers in the food chain, reptiles also act as dispersers for various plant species, as is the case with some species of lizard. In addition to their ecological importance, several reptile species also have socio-economic importance, especially some chelonians, which serve as food for human populations. And the venomous snakes whose venoms give rise to the antihypertensive drug Captopril (MARTINS et al., 2003), and EVASIN, recently patented by researchers at the Butantan Institute in São Paulo. Another new drug is ENPAK, a protein with analgesic power much more potent than morphine extracted from the venom of the rattlesnake, *Crotallus durissus terrificus* (BERNARDE, 2013).

In the fourth question, which asked what you feel when you see or hear about frogs, snakes, turtles and alligators, three stereotypes were established: neutral, positive and negative. Neutral was defined when the answers were **"nothing"**, while the other feelings were grouped between positive and negative.

With regard to feelings towards frogs (Graph 4), 52 per cent of the participants view

22

frogs negatively, and the most common expressions used to describe their feelings towards these animals are: *I'm* **scared**, **I'm terrified of frogs, I'm allergic**, *I'm disgusted*, *it's* **strange and cold, I'm scared and disgusted, I'm at risk of catching it, and** only 7 per cent of the expressions were positive, among them: I'm **calm and I can catch it**. Of the other 41 per cent, 31 per cent of the feelings fall under Neutral: **nothing, I don't feel anything,** and the other 10 per cent didn't answer.

comment on how you feel when you see or hear a frog:

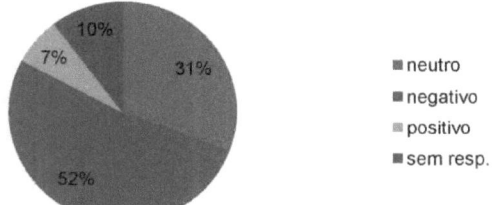

Graph 4. Classification of the perceptions of toads held by public school students in Serra Talhada, Pernambuco, (n=29), (question 4).

When asked how they feel when they see or hear about snakes, the negative expressions were expressed in various ways such as: **fear**, **I'm afraid**, **fear and phobia, very afraid, poisonous and dangerous, fright, suspense, disgust,** etc. totalling 52% of the responses, as shown in Graph 5. The only positive perception was from student 3, *"beautiful"*.

comment on how you feel when you see or hear about snakes

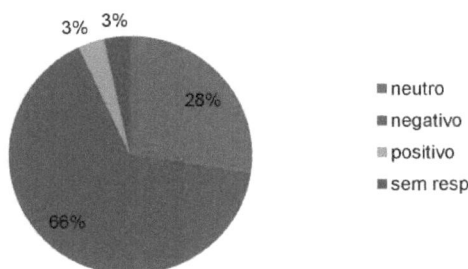

Graph 5. Classification of the perceptions of snakes held by public school students in Serra Talhada, Pernambuco (n=29) (question 4).

Snakes are seen in a very negative light, with fear being the main feeling aroused by them (52 per cent). According to Alves and his colleagues (2012), most societies are ophidiophobic, i.e. they perceive snakes as cruel creatures with a deep hatred of human beings. In this case, the acceptance of a negative stereotype is common, as people believe that all snakes are dangerous and pose some risk to humans, probably due to religious influence and the spread of legends/myths over time. However, only 15 per cent of Brazilian species are of medical importance (MOURA et al., 2010).

Snakes have long been an object of fear and superstition for humanity. However, they were venerated and worshipped by many primitive peoples. In addition, many erroneous beliefs about them still persist in civilised countries, despite the wealth of current knowledge about their biology as well as their place in nature as a group of predatory animals (STORER et al., 2003).

Cardoso and colleagues (2010) carried out an ethnoherpetological approach to find out what the residents of some municipalities in the southern half of the state of Rio Grande do Sul know about snakes. The data obtained was analysed by the group, and the reports showed that the population has some knowledge related to snakes. This knowledge is

empirical, since all the interviewees showed some misconceptions, which the group considered to be myths.

Perrelli and colleagues (2010) sought to identify indigenous knowledge and practices in relation to snakes and to reflect on environmental education in this context. According to the results obtained, the authors realised that some of the practices reported cause damage to the environment and compromise people's lives.

With regard to turtles, as can be **seen in** Graph 6, the majority of expressions, 38 per cent, were positive, including: **beautiful, I like to see them, delicate, I like them, I even pick them up, I like them, I'm not afraid, they're cute,** only 10 per cent were negative: **I'm afraid, I think they're ugly, slow,** and 38 per cent were neutral: **nothing, a normal animal, I've never seen them.**

comment on what you feel when you see or hear about a turtle

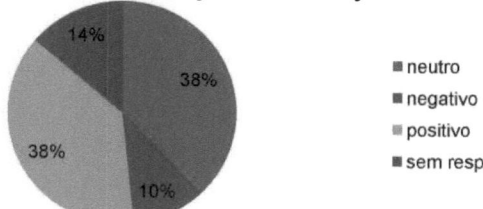

Graph 6. Classification of perceptions of turtles by students in the Youth and Adult Education programme of the public school system in Serra Talhada, Pernambuco (n=29) (Question 4).

Turtles stand out for their positive outlook and sense of fragility. However, the animal that seems to be the biggest villain is the alligator with no positive ratings and 72% of negative expressions, such as: afraid, **I'm afraid, I'm very afraid, angry, dangerous predator, scared, scary.** Of the other 28 per cent, 21 per cent of the expressions were neutral: **nothing, I don't know, I've never seen.** The other 7 per cent didn't answer.

comment on what you feel when you see or hear about alligators:

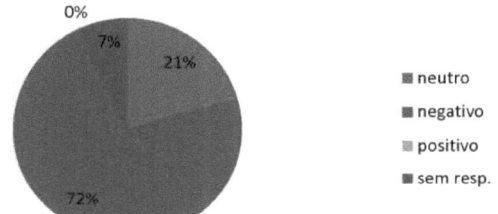

Graph 7. Classification of the perceptions of alligators held by Youth and Adult Education students from schools A and B in Serra Talhada, Pernambuco (Question 4).

When the students were asked if they had ever witnessed someone mistreating one of the representatives of the two groups (fifth question), 55 per cent of the answers were positive, 42 per cent were negative and 4 per cent didn't answer, as shown in graph 8.

have you ever seen anyone mistreating this type of animal?

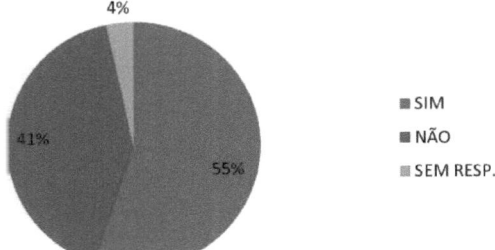

Graph 8. Classification of the perceptions of Youth and Adult Education students from schools A and B in Serra Talhada, Pernambuco (Question 4).

In the fourth question, which asked about the mistreatment they had witnessed, 45 per cent of the participants didn't answer, 27 per cent didn't do anything and the other 28 per cent showed that they didn't like it and even tried to stop it: "**no**

I liked seeing it because animals are just like children, they don't know anything"; "I explained that each animal has its own way of defending itself"; "I pushed the frog with a broom to make it go away"; "I fought, I don't like that kind of attitude"; "I

stopped it", according to graph 9.

What did you do?

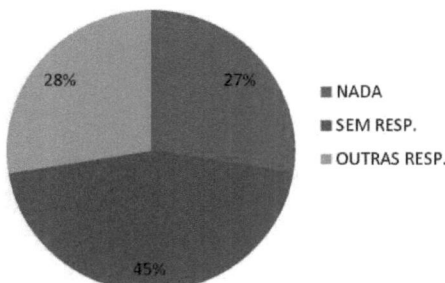

■ NADA
■ SEM RESP.
▩ OUTRAS RESP.

Graph 9. Reactions and attitudes taken to the mistreatment of amphibians and reptiles by EJA students in schools A and B in Serra Talhada, Pernambuco (Question 5).

In question 6, which asked why frogs sing when it rains, 10.3 per cent considered alternative **A to be** correct, 79.3 per cent of the participants correctly indicated alternative **B** (to attract the attention of the female in order to start the reproduction process), and the other 10 per cent indicated alternative **D as** correct, as shown in graph 10.

why do frogs sing when it rains?
■ Série1 ■ Série2

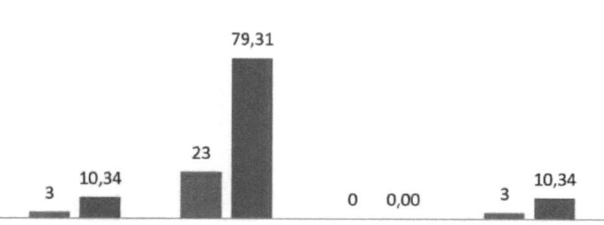

A   B   C   D
Graph 10 - Knowledge of amphibian vocalisations when it rains, by students of Youth and Adult Education in the public school system of Serra Talhada, Pernambuco (n = 29) (Question 6) Legend: A) Act as trophic controllers and bio-indicators; B) Transmit diseases to humans; C) Present threats to humans; D) Don't know.

There are different types of song: announcement song, nuptial song, territorial song, meeting song, reciprocity song, separation song, agony song (KINDEL, 1997; BERNARDE, 2012).

One of the most obvious characteristics of the reproduction of anuran amphibians is the vocalisation of the male to attract the female during reproductive congregations.

26

However, in a rainy summer season, there may be more than ten species of anurans vocalising and reproducing, and singing becomes a mechanism to avoid amplexus (nuptial embrace) between different species (Photo 3), as each female recognises the song of the males of her respective species (BERNARDE, 2012).

Figure 4 - Pair of bathroom frogs - *Scinax duartei* in amplexo for spawning. Source: Ra_bugio.blog.

Anurans breed in aquatic environments, with species preferring lentic environments (still water: ponds, lakes and marshes) and others lotic environments (running water: rivers, streams, brooks, springs, etc.), or choosing between permanent and temporary environments.Vocalisation sites are the environments in which males sing to attract females and each species has its own preferred vocalisation sites, such as on the ground, near a puddle; among grasses; floating in water; partially submerged in water; among sticks; among bushes; on rocks; inside holes in trees; in bromeliads, etc. Most anurans show vocalisation activity during the hottest and rainiest months of the year, but a few species may prefer the dry season (BERNARDE, 2012).

When the male vocalises, he doesn't always attract females; sometimes he can attract a predator or another male who wants to dispute territory (BERNARDE, 2012).

The vocalisation of anuran amphibians is the basis of the reproductive cycle. Based on this concept and knowing that each species has a specific song, it is worth working on this subject in the classroom, especially pointing out the importance of song in the group's reproductive biology, adaptations and all the biological and ecological aspects related to them (KINDEL, 1997).

When asked about the occurrence of amphibians at night (Question 7), the majority of participants, 31 per cent, said that frogs and toads come out at night to feed, 10 per cent said it was for reproduction, 13 per cent said it was to protect themselves from the sun, of the other 46 per cent, 37 per cent didn't answer and another 9 per cent gave other statements, such as: **because at night they don't feel threatened by human beings; because they don't like light; they feel afraid, as shown in** Graph 11.

Explain why frogs and toads occur at night:

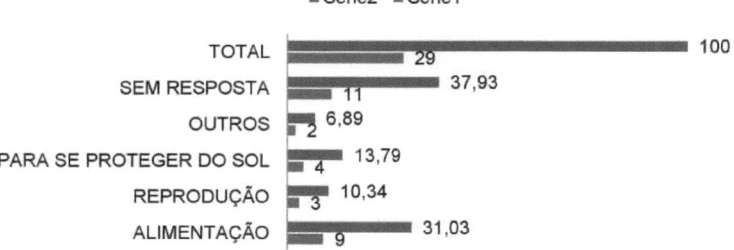

Graph 11 - Students' awareness of the occurrence of amphibians at night in public schools in Serra Talhada, Pernambuco (n= 29) (Question 7).

The occurrence of frogs and toads at night can be explained by a number of reasons, one of which is feeding: the kuru toad (*Rhinella icterica*, *R. marina* and *R. schneideri*) usually approaches the lights of lampposts and houses at night, attracted by the concentration of insects (an example of the importance of amphibians in nature because they consume arthropods). They are harmless animals, despite the belief that they can urinate and blind a person, something that is not beyond the rich imagination of our people. Another factor that must be taken into account is the fact that amphibians have extremely sensitive skin, lined with mucous membranes and also have cutaneous respiration, in which case they need a humid, cool environment and protection from the sun's rays so that their skin doesn't dry out (BERNARDE, 2012).

In question 8, which asked about the diet of amphibians and reptiles, 31 per cent answered that amphibians and reptiles feed only on insects, 17 per cent answered that amphibians and reptiles feed on insects and fruit respectively, 27 per cent answered that amphibians and reptiles feed on: **plants, meat, fruit and bugs; leaves, insects and meat; insects and lizards; small mammals and small insects; leaves and fruit.**

What do amphibians and reptiles eat?

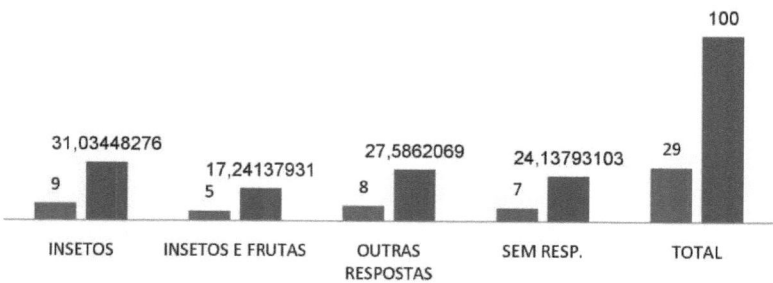

Graph 12: Students' knowledge of amphibian and reptile feeding in public schools in Serra Talhada, Pernambuco (n= 29) (Question 8).

All the amphibian species are carnivores, except for the tree frog *Xenohyla truncata* (photo 4), which feeds on small fruits and is found on sandbanks in the state of Rio de Janeiro. Arthropods (insects and spiders) are the main food item for anurans, but they also prey on other groups, including vertebrates.

Figure 5: Tree frog *Xenohyla truncata*. Photo: Mark Moffeitt/ Minden pictures. Source: National Geographic.

Most lizards feed on arthropods, but there are also species that prey on other animal groups, including vertebrates, as well as herbivorous and omnivorous lizards.

Snakes, unlike anurans and lizards, prey on various animal groups. All species are carnivores that swallow their prey whole and can hunt on various types of substrates (aquatic, subterranean, terrestrial and arboreal). The absence of the sternum bone and the weakly connected jaws, allowing the mouth to open wide, allow these animals to ingest large diameter prey (BERNARDE, 2012).

In question 9, which asked about the eye-catching colouring that some species of amphibians and reptiles have, 62% of the students said that amphibians and reptiles have eye-catching colouring to ward off predators, 34.4% said that amphibians and reptiles have eye-catching colouring to attract females, and the other almost 4% couldn't answer, as shown in graph 13:

Many frogs, snakes and lizards are brightly coloured, why is this?

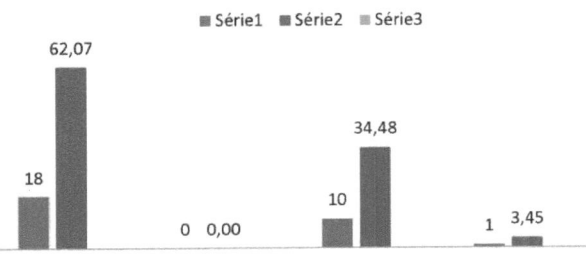

Graph 13. Recognition of the eye-catching colouring of amphibians and reptiles by students of Youth and Adult Education in the public school system of Serra Talhada, Pernambuco, (n=29), (Question 9). Caption: A) To ward off predators; B) To be used as pets; C) To attract the attention of the female; D) I don't know.

Aposematic colouration, also known as warning colouration, is an adaptive characteristic of some animals and plants (venomous or poisonous) that use strong, vivid colours to warn possible predators of their toxicity. These contrasting colours are easily noticeable and are usually related to the presence of some dangerous attribute in the animal, such as toxins in the skin or the ability to inoculate venom, as is the case with some amphibians and reptiles (JARED & ANTONIAZZI, 2009).

Among amphibians, bright colours, which serve as a real warning sign of toxicity, are an effective way of avoiding predation. This is the case with dendrobatids (Photo 5). As we know, dendrobatids are brightly coloured amphibians known for their efficient chemical defence.

Figure 6: Dentrobatidae. A) *Phyllobates terribiliss*. Image source: Google images.B) *Dendrobates azureus*.Image source: Google images. C) *Oophaga pumilio*.Photo: Todd W. Pierson.

The dendrobatids make up a family of around 164 species, distributed throughout South America (mainly the Amazon) and Central America. They are amphibians that stand out for their variety of colours, which generally contrast strongly with the environment in which they live. This is a visual (aposematic) danger signal, very similar to the sound emitted by the rattlesnake's rattle which, translated into our language, would mean something like: danger, don't come any closer!

Like dendrobatid amphibians, some snakes and lizards also have aposematic colouring, an example of which are true corals (Fig. 7), so named because they are venomous and belong to the *Elapidae* family, which have predominantly red colouring, this colouring being a form of defence mechanism against potential predators (BERNARDE 2012).

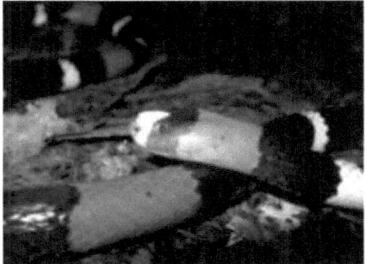

Figura 7   True coral (*Micrurus lemniscatus*). Photo: Paulo Sérgio Bernarde. Source: Herpetofauna.com.

False corals (fig. 8) are so called because they are not venomous and are not involved in serious snakebite accidents. They belong to the *Aniliidae*, *Colubridae* and *Dipsadidae*. The defence mechanism that occurs in false corals is known as mimicry, where the colour pattern can confuse possible predators because they look like real corals

Figura 8   False coral from the Dipsadidae family (*Erythrolamprus aesculapii*). Photo: Daniel Velho. Source: Herpetofauna.com.

In question 10, the aim was to find out a little about knowledge, legends and beliefs relating to amphibians and reptiles, where 75.86% considered that the age of the rattlesnake, *Crotallusdurissus*, is measured by counting the rings of the rattle on the end of its tail and only 13.79% considered this information to be false and 10.34 did not know how to answer, as shown in graph 14:

The age of a rattlesnake can be measured by counting the rings on the rattle

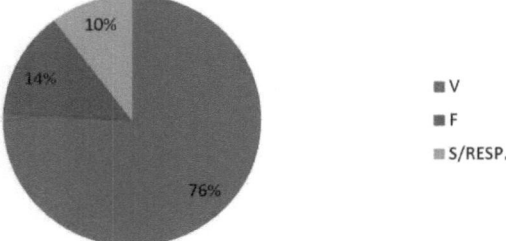

- V
- F
- S/RESP.

Graph 14. Knowledge of legends and beliefs relating to amphibians and reptiles among students in Youth and Adult Education in the public school system in Serra Talhada, Pernambuco, (n=29). Legend: The age of the rattlesnake can be measured by counting the rings on the rattle.

The rattlesnake is a snake of the genus *Crotalus* (Photo 8 A), belonging to the *Viperidae* family. This snake has a terrestrial and nocturnal habit and solenoglyphic teeth (Photo 8 B), making it venomous.

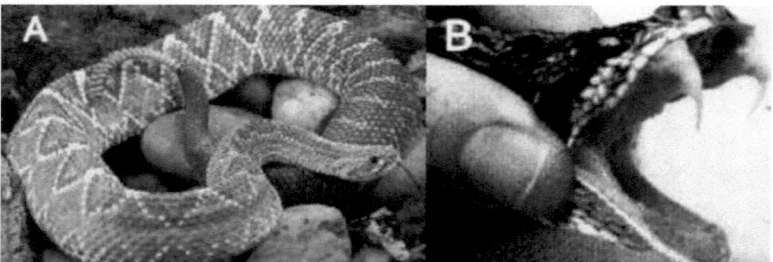

Figure 9. A) Rattlesnake. Photo: google images. B) Type of teeth present in rattlesnakes. Photo: google images.

The most peculiar feature of this species is at the end of its tail, where the rattle is found (Photo 9), an attachment of the integument, with a flat cylindrical shape and made up of hollow rings which, like the scales, are made up of keratin, a protein that also makes up our hair and nails (PINHEIRO, 2009; BERNARDE, 2012).

Figura 10 Detail of the rattlesnake's tail showing the rattle. Photo: google images.

Snake scales can have different shapes, sizes and textures and are adapted for specific functions. One of the most notable adaptations is seen in rattlesnakes, which have a caudal appendage, the rattle, formed by modifications to the scales and which also involves fusion of the last caudal vertebrae (Photo 10), forming a single piece, the style, into which the muscles that move it are inserted (MELGAREJO, 2009).

A common behaviour exhibited by rattlesnakes, according to Pinheiro (2009), is to vibrate their tails when they feel threatened, causing the rings that make up the rattle to clash, emitting a characteristic sound to scare away possible predators (Photo 11).

Figura 11   Cascavel shaking the rattle in defence. Photo: Luan Pinheiro. Source: NUROF blog.

Many people believe that the number of rings on the rattlesnake's rattle is related to the snake's age, with each ring corresponding to a different age.

year of the animal's life. So a rattlesnake with a rattle made up of seven rings would be seven years old. This belief has spread throughout Brazil, saying that each ring of the rattle corresponds to one year of the rattlesnake's life, which in reality corresponds to the number of times the snake has changed its skin (moulted) and many rings also end up being lost throughout the animal's life (PINHEIRO, 2011).

65.52 per cent considered it false that snakes can hear and 24.14 per cent considered it true and another 10.34 per cent didn't know how to answer, graph 16:

Snakes can hear

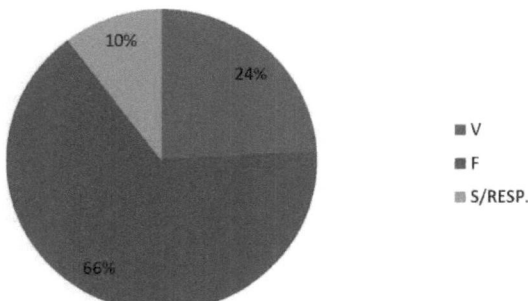

- V
- F
- S/RESP.

Graph 15. Knowledge of legends and beliefs relating to amphibians and reptiles among students in Youth and Adult Education in the public school system in Serra Talhada, Pernambuco, (n=29). Caption: Snakes can hear.

Contrary to many who believe that snakes can hear, their ability to hear airborne sounds is practically non-existent, due to the lack of an outer and middle ear. The inner ear is connected by a delicate bony structure, the columella, to the square bone, which articulates with the mandible. This characteristic gives snakes a particular sensitivity to the vibrations of the substrate on which they are found (MELGAREREJO, 2009).

Because of this hearing impairment, snakes have developed other mechanisms to fulfil their needs, such as: The sense of smell, which is quite acute in these animals, and which varies according to the habits of each group. This sense is not related to the presence of the epithelium of the nasal cavities, which seem to be responsible only for conditioning and conducting the air for breathing. Alternatively, by means of vibrating movements of the thin, long tongue, the snake scans for particles suspended in the air, which the forked end conducts to Jacobson's organ, a specialised chemoreceptor structure, lined with sensory epithelium, located in the anterior region of the roof of the mouth. Thermoreception is another adaptation present in the boidae and viperidae families, which makes it easier to detect, approach and capture food. Boids have sensory adaptations in the supra- and infralabial scales which, in some cases, form labial fossae, as shown in photo 12.

Figura 12 Details of the labial fossettes in the boideae, *Coralus caninus*. Source: google images.

Looking in more detail at the organs found in viperids, the loreal fossae, photo 13, are characteristic of the Crotalinae subfamily, as these structures are important for quickly identifying these snakes, which cause 99% of accidents in Brazil. The loreal fossa is located slightly below the line separating the eye from the nostril, on each side of the face, and is contained in a cavity in the maxillary bone (MELGAREREJO, 2009).

Figura 13   Detail of the loreal fossa in the viperidae, *Bohtropsinsularis*. Source: google images

58.62 per cent think it's true that when a lizard loses a piece of its tail it has the ability to grow another one in its place, 27.59 per cent think it's false and 13.79 per cent couldn't answer, Graph 17:

When a lizard loses a piece of its tail, it has the ability to grow a new one

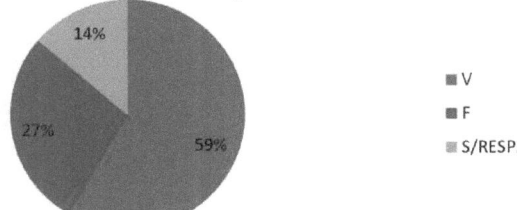

■ V
■ F
▧ S/RESP.

Graph 16. Knowledge of legends and beliefs relating to amphibians and reptiles among students in Youth and Adult Education in the public school system in Serra Talhada, Pernambuco, (n=29). Legend: When a lizard loses a piece of its tail, it has the ability to grow a new one.

Amphibians and reptiles display several different types of defence behaviour and these behavioural strategies are used in the different phases of predation, an example of which is tail autotomisation, which consists of the ability to drop the tail when captured by a predator, and which occurs in most lizards. Autotomising the tail is a way of escaping predators, used by

several species of lizard (Photo 14 A). The broken tail remains in motion for a while, which helps to distract the predator and help the lizard escape. The tail regenerates in several species (Photo 14 B), but during this time the animal has to bear the consequences, such

35

as reduced body growth and decreased locomotion capacity or even lower reproductive success (BERNARDE, 2012).

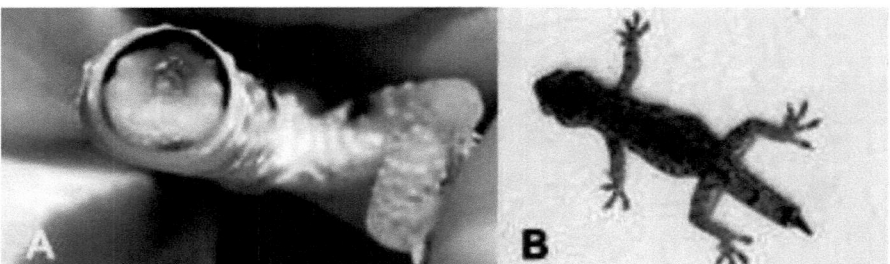

Figure 14. A. Detail of lizard tail after autotomisation. **B**. Individual with tail in regeneration stage. Source: google images.

68.97 per cent considered the statement *"coral snake stings with its tail"* to be false, while 17.24 per cent considered it to be true and 13.79 were unable to answer, Graph 18:

The coral snake stings with its tail

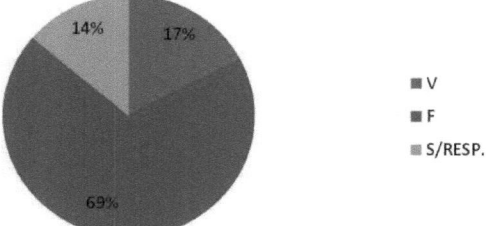

Graph 17. Knowledge of legends and beliefs relating to amphibians and reptiles among students in Youth and Adult Education in the public school system in Serra Talhada, Pernambuco, (n=29).
Caption: The coral snake stings with its tail.

Legend has it that the true coral (*Elapidae*) has a venomous stinger at the end of its tail. The explanation for this, according to Bernarde (2012), may lie in the observation that these snakes have a relatively short and thick tail (figure 15 A), as well as the behaviour of curling up and raising the tip of the tail (figures 13 B and 15 C) as a defence mechanism, thus giving the impression that the posterior region of the body is the head. In this case, those unfamiliar with this snake's habits are left with the impression that it has a stinger capable of inoculating venom through its tail.

Figure 15. A) True coral (Micrurus ibiboboca) - typical of the Northeast. Photo: Willianilson Pessoa. Source: Herpetofauna.com; B) True coral (*Micrurus surinamensis*), flattening its body dorso-ventrally and showing its tail. Source: Herpetofauna.com; C) True coral (Micrurus ssp) showing its tail in defence. Source: Herpetofauna.com.

With regard to toad urine, 55.17% of the participants considered it true that sack urine blinds, while 27.59% considered the statement false and the other 17.24% were unable to answer (Graph 20).

Blind toad urine

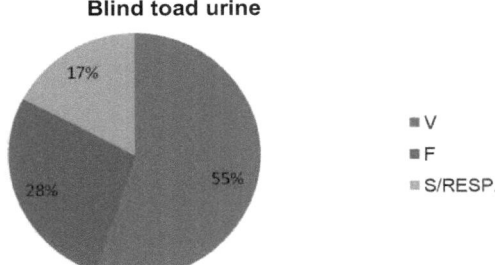

■ V
■ F
▩ S/RESP.

Graph 18. Knowledge of legends and beliefs relating to amphibians and reptiles among students in Youth and Adult Education in the public school system in Serra Talhada, Pernambuco, (n=29). Caption: Blind toad urine.

The idea that toad urine is a dangerous poison that can lead to blindness is still very common. It is seen in the popular imagination as a cunning animal that is capable of targeting the eyes of its victims and splashing its terrible urine on them. According to Bernarde (2012), some say that the urine of the toad (*Rhinella icterica, R. marina and R. schneideri*) blinds, but in fact the toad may urinate as a defence mechanism when fleeing and the urine would not cause problems "if" it hit someone's eyes. The "milk" corresponds to the poison contained in the paratoid glands, located dorsally behind the animal's eyes (Photo 16). The toad won't be able to project this poison onto a person, but if these glands are compressed, the poison can be thrown a short distance. I know of two cases of children who were hitting toads and the poison splashed into their eyes, which caused discomfort in their vision and passed after they washed their eyes.

Figure 16 - View of the paratoid gland in the Kururu toad (*Rhinella marina*), located behind the animal's eyes. Source: Herpetofauna.

10.9 51.72 per cent considered it true that the frog is the female of the male, while 34.48 per cent considered it false and 13.79 per cent were unable to answer, as shown in graph 21.

The frog is the female frog

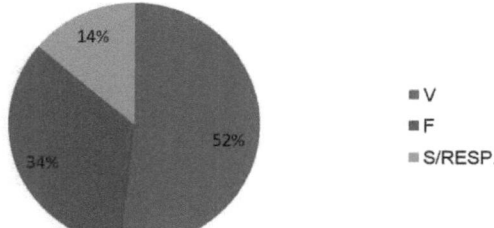

- V
- F
- S/RESP.

Graph 19. Knowledge of legends and beliefs relating to amphibians and reptiles among students in Youth and Adult Education in the public school system in Serra Talhada, Pernambuco, (n=29). Legend: The frog is the female of the toad.

Although interest in amphibians has been growing in recent years, there is a lot of misinformation about them. Many errors are commonly propagated about their biology and classification, the most common being the popular concept that the frog is the female of the toad. In order to clarify the fact that many people confuse the frog with the toad, it is necessary to highlight the biological and behavioural differences, as well as the classification of anuran amphibians. Anuran amphibians are divided into three large groups: toads, frogs and tree frogs. The frog group (Photo 17) is made up of very bulky, terrestrial animals that generally have rough, drier skin compared to frogs and toads. They have a pair of glandular protuberances behind their eyes known as parotoid glands (Photo 16);

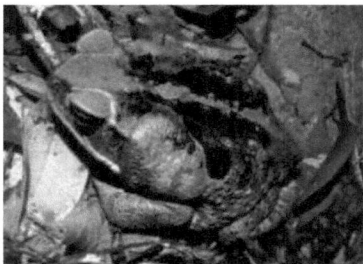

Figure 17 - Kururu toad (*Rhinella marina*). Photo: Paulo Sérgio Bernarde. Source: Herpetofauna.

The other group is the frogs (Photo 17), which are animals associated with humid or aquatic environments. Their skin is very smooth and moist, they have tapered toes and their locomotion is fast, with long jumps;

Figure 18 - Peppered frog (*Leptodactylus labyrinthicus*). Photo: Paulo Sérgio Bernarde.Source: Herpetofauna.

And finally, the group of peregrines (Photo 18), which are characterised by having adhesive discs on their fingertips, giving them the ability to move around in vegetation or on walls. In general, they also have smooth, moist skin and can make great leaps, which justifies their name which, according to the Houaiss dictionary, comes from the Tupi *pere'reg and* means "to jump".

Figura 19 Perereca (Scinax ruber). Photo by Paulo S. Bernarde. Source: Herpetofauna.

CHAPTER 5

FINAL CONSIDERATIONS

With regard to the classification of amphibians, there was a misunderstanding, especially in relation to Cecilias, which many claimed was a people's name, so they didn't know if it was part of the group in question. However, it is believed that this was mainly because Cecilia are fossorial and are popularly known as blind snakes. With regard to the classification of reptiles, although the majority chose the correct alternative, their knowledge of the two-headed snake as a reptile cannot be proven, as at least five participants were asked during the survey whether two-headed snakes exist. The majority recognise that amphibians and reptiles act as pest controllers.

Snakes, lizards, frogs and alligators are seen in a very negative light, arousing feelings of fear, disgust and loathing, while turtles stand out for their positive outlook and sense of fragility, to which feelings of pity, tenderness and affection were attributed.

There is still a huge deficiency in the teaching of zoology, especially on the subject in question, which results in a lack of knowledge about aspects of the ecology and biology of these animals. It is also worth emphasising that some very old myths are present in the daily lives of students, contributing to the formation of a mistaken view of herpetofauna.

In this way, we can see that the participants in the survey have considerable knowledge about amphibians and reptiles. However, there is still the influence of certain legends that make up this learning, and it is necessary to elucidate these themes within the science disciplines, especially in the early grades, as well as to bring students closer to the reality that surrounds them, through changes in the profile of science classes, confronting scientific and traditional knowledge. We also believe that universities, especially teacher training colleges, can work intensively within schools, making improvements to degree programmes or creating partnerships with schools and biology teachers.

CHAPTER 6

BIBLIOGRAPHICAL REFERENCES

ADAMS, C. **Caiçaras in the Atlantic Forest: research versus environmental planning and management.** Annablume: FAPESP. São Paulo. 2000. 337p.

ANDRADE-LIMA, D. Vegetation. In: National Atlas of Brazil. IBGE/National Council of Geography, 1966.

ANDRADE-LIMA, D. The caatingas dominium. Revista Brasileira de Botânica. 4: 149-153, 1981.

BARBOSA, A. R. NISHIDA, A. K.; COSTA, E. S.; CASÉ, A. L. R. Ethnoherpetological approach to São José da Mata - Paraíba - Brazil. **Revista de Biologia e Ciência da Terra.** 2007; 7(2): 117-123.

BARBOSA, R. N.; MOTA, B. A. E.; SANTOS, E. M. Environmental Education: An experience in a school. In: Mata da Pimenteira State Park: Natural Wealth and Conservation of the Caatinga. 1 ed. v. 1, EDUFRPE: Recife, 2013. 257p.

BÉRNILS, R.S., J.C. Moura-Leite and S.A.A. Morato. 2004. Reptiles, p.497-535. In: S.B. Mikich& R.S. Bérnils (org.). Red Book of Threatened Fauna in the State of Paraná. Curitiba: Environmental Institute of Paraná. 764p.

BERNARDE, P. S. **Curiosities about snakes.** Available at: <http://www.herpetofauna.com.br/curiosidades_sobre_as_cobras.htm>. Accessed on: 16 May 2015.

BERNARDE, P. S. **Amphibians and reptiles: introduction to the study of Brazilian herpetofauna.**1 ed. v.1. Anolisbooks Editora: Curitiba, 2012. Xxp.

BRAZIL. Secretariat of Basic Education. National Curriculum Parameters: Introduction to the National Curriculum Parameters - Brasília: MEC/SEF, 1997. 126p.

BRAZIL. National Curriculum Parameters: Secondary Education. 2000. Brasília: MEC/SEF. 109p.

BRAZIL. Secretariat of Mines and Metallurgy. Ministry of Mines and Energy: Geological Survey of Brazil. Brazil, 2008.

BRAZIL. Ministry of the Environment. Law No. 9.795/1999. Provides for environmental education, institutes the National Environmental Education Policy and makes other provisions. Available at: <http://www.mma.gov.br/port/conama/legiabre.cfm?codlegi=321>. Accessed on: 14 Nov. 2015.

BONI, V. QUARESMA, S. J. Aprendendo a entrevistar: como fazer entrevistas em Ciências Sociais. In Thesis. Revista Eletrônica dos PósGraduação em Sociologia Política da UFSC, Santa Catarina, Vol. 2, n. 1 (3), p. 68-80, jan./jul. 2005.

CARDOSO, C. C. RABELATO, M. M.; FERREIRA, L. D. MARINHO, J. C.B.; SOARES, G. C.; SANTORI, J. **Ethnoherpetological analysis of snakes: influence on biology teaching.** XI Scientific Initiation Exhibition - PUCRS - 2010.

COSTA-NETO, E. M. Etnozoologia no Brasil: um panorama bibliográfico. **Revista Bioikos.** 2000; 14(2.): 31-45.PUC-Campinas-SP. 2000.

CHALITA, Gabriel. Education: the solution lies in affection. São Paulo: Gente, 2002.

DIAS, G. F. **Environmental education:** principles and practices. 9.ed. São Paulo: Gaia, 2004.

DIEGUES, A. C; ARRUDA, R. S. U; SILVA, U. C. F; FIGOLS, F. A. B; ANDRADE, D. Ministério do Meio, Dos Recursos Hídricos e Amazônia Legal. Traditional knowledge and biodiversity in Brazil.COBIO,NUPUB, University of São Paulo, São Paulo,SP,1999.

DUELLMAN, W. E. & TRUEB., L. 1994.Biology of Amphibians. Baltimore, The Johns Hopkins University Press, 670p.

FERREIRA, H. F.; CRUZ, R. L.; BORJES-NOJOSA, D. M.; ALVES, R. R. N. Beliefs associated with snakes in the state of Ceará, Northeast Brazil. **Sitientibus Journal: Biological Sciences Series.** 11(2): 153-163. 2011.

SERRA TALHADA HOUSE OF CULTURE FOUNDATION - FCCST. **The history of Serra Talhada.** Available at: <http://www.fundacaocasadacultura.com.br/site/?p=materias_ver&materia=1>. Accessed on: 01 October 2015.

GIL, A. C. Como elaborar projetos de pesquisa. 5. ed. São Paulo: Atlas, 2008.

GUEDES, J. C. S. **Environmental education in primary schools: a case study.** Garanhuns: Ed. doautor, 2006.

HICKMAN C., ROBERTS L., LARSON A. **Integrated Principles of Zoology.** 11th edition. Guanabara Koogan, Rio de Janeiro. 2004. ISBN 85-277-0868-X

BRAZILIAN INSTITUTE OF GEOGRAPHY AND STATISTICS - IBGE. **Census Demographic 2010.** Available at: <http://www.cidades.ibge.gov.br/painel/painel.php?lang=&codmun=261390&search= %7Cserra-talhada>. Accessed on: 06 October 2015.

KINDEL, E. A. I. WORTMANN, M. L. SOUZA, N. G. S. Studying amphibians in an urban environment. In: WORTMANN, M. L et al., (org.) O estudo dos vertebrados na Escola Fundamental. São Leopoldo: Ed. Unisinos, 1997. 132p.

KURY, C. R. J. Basic education in Brazil. Educ. Soc., Campinas, vol. 23, n. 80, September/2002, p. 168-200

LAKATUS, E. M. MARCONI, M. A. Metodologia do trabalho científico: procedimentos básicos, pesquisa bibliográfica, projeto e relatório, publicações e trabalhos científicos. 5. ed. São Paulo: Atlas, 2003.

JARED & ANTONIAZZI

LEAL, I.R.; TABARELLI, M.; SILVA, J.M.C. da. Ecology and conservation of the caatinga. Recife: UFPE. 2003.

LIMA, W. Learning and social classification: a challenge to concepts. **Fórum Crítico da Educação**: Revista do ISEP/Programa de Mestrado em Ciências Pedagógicas. v. 3, n. 1, oct. 2004.

LUCHESE, M. S. **A Herpetologia no Ensino Fundamental:o que os alunos pensam e aprendem.**[Monografia] Universidade federal do Rio Grande do Sul, Instituto de Biociências - Comissão de Graduação em Ciências Biológicas, Porto Alegre, 2013.

MAFFEI, F. Diversity and habitat use of anuran amphibian communities in Lençóis Paulista, State of São Paulo- Botucatu : [s.n.]. Dissertation (master's degree) - Universidade Estadual Paulista, Instituto de Biociências, Botucatu, 2010.

MARTINS NETO, S.F. **Fragile matrix composite material reinforced with natural sisal and mallow fibres: characterisation and correlation of mechanical properties.** 2011. (Dissertation in Mechanical Engineering). Department of Mechanical Engineering, Federal University of Pará, Belém. 2011.

MARTINS, M.; MOLINA, F. B.; **Reptiles.** In: MACHADO, A. B.;DRUMMOND, G. M.; PAGLIA, A. P. (Eds). **Red Book of Endangered Brazilian Fauna.** Brasílis: MMA, Belo Horizonte: Biodiversitas Foundation, 2008. 2V. 1420p.

MELGAREJO. A. R. 2003. Venomous snakes in Brazil. Pp. 33-61 In: Venomous animals in Brazil: biology, clinic and therapeutics of accidents. Cardoso et al. (eds.). Sarvier, São Paulo - SP

MINAYO, M. C. S. (org.). **Pesquisa Social**: teoria, método e criatividade. 31 ed. Petrópolis, RJ: Vozes, 2012.

42

MOURA, M.R.; COSTA, H.C.; SÃO-PEDRO, V. A.; FERNANDES, V.D.; FEIO, R. N. The relationship between people and snakes in eastern Minas Gerais, southeastern Brazil. Biota Neotropica (Portuguese Edition. Online), v. 10, p. 133-141,2010.

OLIVEIRA, H. T. Popular education and environmental education in Latin America: converging paths and aspirations. In: GONZALES-GAUDIANO, E., Environmental education identily, politics and citizenship. Rotterdam, the Netherlands: Sense publishers, 2008. P. 219 - 230.

PERRELLI, M. A. S. SANTA-RITA,P. H; CONTINI, A. Z. **Traditional knowledge about snakes and implications for intercultural environmental education.**Série-Estudos- periodical of the postgraduate programme in Education at UCDB, Campo Grande-MS, 2010.

POSEY, D. Introduction - Ethnobiology: theory and practice. In: RIBEIRO, B. (Ed.) Suma Etnológica Brasileira. Ethnobiology. Petrópolis: Vozes, 1987. v. 1. p. 15-25.

REIGOTA, M. What is environmental education? 1.ed. São Paulo: Brasiliense, 2001.

ROCHA-COELHO, F. B. O uso das plantas no cotidiano da comunidade quilombola Kalunga do Mimoso - Tocantins: um estudo Etnobotânico. Dissertation (Master's Programme in Environmental Sciences) PGCiamb, Federal University of Tocantins, Tocantins, 2009.

RODRIGUES, M. T. Herpetofauna of the Caatinga. In: Leal, I.R.,Tabarelli, M. & Silva, J.M.C. (eds.), Ecologia e Conservação da Caatinga. Editora Universitária, UFPE, 275-333 pp. 2003.

RODRIGUES, A. S. L. Are global conservation efforts successful? Science, V.313, p. 1052 - 1052, 2007.

ROSA, M. D.**os fungos na escola:** análise dos conteúdos de micologia em livros didáticos do ensino fundamental de Florianópolis. 2009. 53 p. Monografia (Bachelor's degree) - Biological sciences course, department of teaching methodology Centre for Educational Sciences, UFSC, Florianópolis, 2009.

SANTOS-FITA, D.; COSTA-NETO, E. M. Interactions between humans and animals: the contribution of ethnozoology. **Biotemas,** v. 20, n. 4, dec. 2007.

SANTOS, E. M; MELO JÚNIOR, M; SILVA-CAVALCANTI, J. S; ALMEIDA, G. V. L. Parque Estadual Mata da Pimenteira: Riqueza natural e conservação da caatinga. 1 ed. v. 1, EDUFRPE: Recife, 2013.

STORER, T. I; USINGER R. L; STEBBINS, R. C; NYBAKKEN, J. W. **General Zoology.** 6 ed. v.8, Companhia Editora: São Paulo, 2003.

CHAPTER 7

ANNEXES

Annex 1:

AUTARQUIA EDUCACIONAL DE SERRA TALHADA-AESET FACULDADE DE FORMAÇÃO DE PROFESSORES DE SERRA TALHADA -FAFOPST

LETTER OF ACCEPTANCE FOR MONOGRAPH SUPERVISION SEMESTER 201

I, the lecturer of the (name of course and institution) course, hereby declare that I agree to take on the supervision of the following student

I, a student on the (name of course) course, undertake to meet all the deadlines set for each stage of the final submission of the Monograph and to attend the orientation meetings determined by the research supervisor.

By signing this Term of Commitment, the supervisor and the student being supervised also declare that: they promise to strictly comply with the deadlines set for the delivery of the various stages of the work, as well as to be present at all the meetings planned between the supervising teacher and the student being supervised.

Provisional title of the research project

Supervisor: _____

Guiding: _____

Serra Talhada,from

ANNEX 2.

CONSENT FORM

The Faculty of Teacher Training of Serra Talhada - FAFOPST, located at Av. Afonso Magalhães S/N, Nossa Senhora da Penha, hereby represented by the coordinator of the Degree Course in Biological Sciences, in the person of Professor Ana Paula Sousa Gomes, enter into a partnership agreement with the school with the aim of enabling the Monograph Research of student Ana Lúcia Maria da Silva Gomes, duly enrolled, supervised by Professor Eliete Pereira Viturino.

The period of validity of this research is months, starting from from the date of signature, and may be amended or supplemented by agreement between the parties.

It is agreed that after the end of the research, the results will be passed on to the granting institution as a way of updating and clarifying the data obtained in the research.

Serra Talhada,from

Stamp and signature of the granting unit

Stamp and signature of the coordinator of the
Serra Talhada Teacher Training College
- FAFOPST